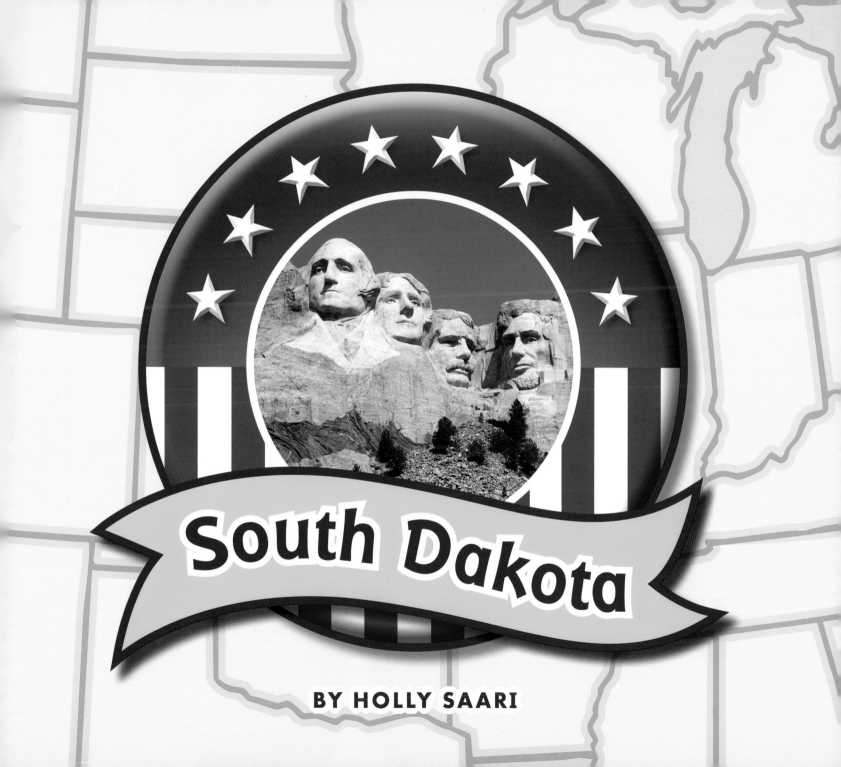

South Dakota

BY HOLLY SAARI

The Child's World

Published by The Child's World®
1980 Lookout Drive • Mankato, MN 56003-1705
800-599-READ • www.childsworld.com

ACKNOWLEDGMENTS
The Child's World®: Mary Berendes, Publishing Director
The Design Lab: Design and production
Red Line Editorial: Editorial direction

PHOTO CREDITS: Jonathan Larsen/Shutterstock Images, cover, 1, 3; Matt
Kania/Map Hero, Inc., 4, 5; iStockphoto, 7, 9, 10, 17; Lijuan Guo/Shutterstock
Images, 11; John Wollwerth/123RF, 13; Library of Congress, 15; Jim Bourg/
AP Images, 19; Shutterstock Images, 21; One Mile Up, 22; Quarter-dollar
coin image from the United States Mint, 22

LIBRARY OF CONGRESS CATALOGING-IN-PUBLICATION DATA
Saari, Holly.
 South Dakota / by Holly Saari.
    p. cm.
 Includes bibliographical references and index.
 ISBN 978-1-60253-486-5 (library bound : alk. paper)
 1. South Dakota—Juvenile literature. I. Title.

F651.3.S23 2010
978.3—dc22

2010019326

Printed in the United States of America in Mankato, Minnesota.
July 2010
F11538

On the cover:
Mount Rushmore
is located in
Keystone, South
Dakota.

CONTENTS

Geography

Let's explore South Dakota! South Dakota is in the north-central United States. This area is called the Midwest.

MONTANA

NORTH DAKOTA

NORTH
WEST   EAST
SOUTH

MINNESOTA

Lemmon •

Sisseton •

Aberdeen •

SOUTH DAKOTA

• Rapid City

Madison •

Black Hills
National
Forest   Mount Rushmore
National Memorial
• Custer

• Wall   • Philip

Badlands
National Park

Pierre

Mitchell •

Sioux Falls •

• Hot Springs

Missouri River

Vermillion •

IOWA

NEBRASKA

Cities

Pierre is the capital of South Dakota. Sioux Falls is the state's largest city. Rapid City and Aberdeen are other well-known cities.

The South Dakota State Capitol in Pierre was completed in 1910. ▶

Land

The Missouri River runs through the center of South Dakota. The eastern part of the state has **plains**. In the west are low mountains. They are called the Black Hills. The **Badlands** are in the southwest. The ground in this area is bad for farming. The Badlands have colorful cliffs and steep valleys.

The Black Hills became famous when gold was found there in the late 1800s.

In the Badlands, the cliffs are striped with different colors. ▶

Plants and Animals

The Black Hills area has many trees. The state tree is the Black Hills spruce. It is an **evergreen**. The state flower is the pasque. Deer live in all parts of the state. The state bird is the ring-necked pheasant.

The pasque is small and purple. ▶

11

People and Work

More than 780,000 people live in South Dakota. Some people work in **finance**, **tourism**, or mining. Many people work in government jobs or **manufacturing**. A large part of the state's land is used for farming. South Dakota crops include corn and wheat.

Farmers in South Dakota also raise cattle and hogs.

Corn is used to make many products, including corn starch and some types of fuel. ▶

History

People from France explored the South Dakota area in the 1700s. In 1803, the United States bought the land from France. After a railroad was built in the 1870s, more people moved to the area. But many Native Americans had lived there long before then. Battles were fought between these **tribes** and the U.S. Army. The tribes were moved to **reservations**. South Dakota became the fortieth state on November 2, 1889.

Native Americans, including the Lakota tribe, ▶ are a large part of South Dakota's history.

Meriwether Lewis and William Clark explored the South Dakota area in 1804.

Ways of Life

South Dakota has many things to do. Tourists travel here to see the different types of land and animals. They also come here to hunt and fish. People enjoy camping in the state's parks. **Rodeos** are **popular** in the state.

A tourist views the Crazy Horse **Memorial** in the Black Hills. ▶

Famous People

Tom Brokaw was born in South Dakota. He works on television news shows. Crazy Horse was a Native American leader in South Dakota. The Native Americans wanted to guard their land. He helped his people fight against the U.S. Army.

Tom Brokaw was born in Webster, South Dakota. ▶

Famous Places

Mount Rushmore is a well-known place in South Dakota. It is a large memorial on the side of a mountain in the Black Hills. The faces of four presidents are carved in rock. They are George Washington, Thomas Jefferson, Theodore Roosevelt, and Abraham Lincoln.

Mount Rushmore was carved from 1927 to 1941. ▶

State Symbols

Seal

South Dakota's state seal shows a picture of a person farming and a boat on the Missouri River. Go to childsworld.com/links for a link to South Dakota's state Web site, where you can get a firsthand look at the state seal.

Flag

South Dakota's flag says "The Mount Rushmore State." This is the state's nickname.

Quarter

The South Dakota state quarter shows Mount Rushmore and a pheasant. The quarter came out in 2006.

Glossary

Badlands (BAD-landz): Badlands are areas of land with rock formations, few plants, and little soil. The Badlands are an area in southwestern South Dakota.

evergreen (EV-ur-green): An evergreen is a tree that does not lose its leaves. South Dakota's state tree is an evergreen called the Black Hills spruce.

finance (FYE-nanss): Finance is a group of businesses that take care of money. Finance is an important industry in South Dakota.

manufacturing (man-yuh-FAK-chur-ing): Manufacturing is the task of making items with machines. Many people in South Dakota have manufacturing jobs.

memorial (muh-MOR-ee-ul): A memorial is a place or thing that honors people or events. The Crazy Horse Memorial is in South Dakota.

plains (PLAYNZ): Plains are areas of flat land that do not have many trees. Part of South Dakota has plains.

popular (POP-yuh-lur): To be popular is to be enjoyed by many people. Hunting and fishing are popular in South Dakota.

reservations (rez-ur-VAY-shunz): Reservations are areas of land that are saved for a certain use. Some Native Americans in South Dakota live on reservations.

rodeos (ROH-dee-ohz): Rodeos are contests in which people ride horses and rope cattle. Rodeos are popular in South Dakota.

seal (SEEL): A seal is a symbol a state uses for government business. South Dakota's state seal has a picture of a person farming and a boat on the Missouri River.

symbols (SIM-bulz): Symbols are pictures or things that stand for something else. The seal and the flag are South Dakota's symbols.

tourism (TOOR-ih-zum): Tourism is visiting another place (such as a state or country) for fun or the jobs that help these visitors. Tourism is popular in South Dakota.

tribes (TRYBZ): Tribes are groups of people who share ancestors and customs. Native American tribes have lived in the South Dakota area for thousands of years.

Further Information

Books

Keller, Laurie. *The Scrambled States of America*. New York: Henry Holt, 2002.

Martonyi, E. Andrew. *The Little Man In the Map: With Clues To Remember All 50 States*. Woodland Hills, CA: Schoolside Press, 2007.

Thornton, Brian. *The Everything Kids' States Book: Wind Your Way Across Our Great Nation*. Avon, MA: Adams Media, 2007.

Web Sites

Visit our Web site for links about South Dakota: *childsworld.com/links*

Note to Parents, Teachers, and Librarians: We routinely verify our Web links to make sure they are safe and active sites. So encourage your readers to check them out!

Index